Ghosts!
Of Pennsylvania

By Lawrence J. Gavlak

Ghosts Of Pennsylvania

Written By Lawrence J. Gavlak

Cover Design by Lawrence J. Gavlak
and Marcia Gavlak

Published by: LJ Gavlak Publishing
PO Box 72
Kylertown, PA 16847
(814) 345-6391
largav@juno.com

ISBN#0-9740357-3-4

Printed in the United States of America

The author on the Battlefield at Gettysburg

This book is dedicated to all of the friends and family that have gone on to their Heavenly Reward. Namely, John, Joe and Jean Sternesky, Joe Fresh, Elva Hamilton, Betty Jay, Mike Kuhar and numerous aunts and uncles. Also, at the top of my list, I must not forget my parents, Albert Gavlak and Frances Lutz Gavlak who have been missed for quite some time.

However, all thanks must go to our Heavenly Father and His Son. What a beautiful gift of reading and writing You have given to all of us! Thank you!

Table Of Contents

Introduction

Pennsylvania can certainly boast of many famous places within the state that are purportedly haunted by spirits of the past. While compiling material for this book I consistently encountered allegedly true stories of famous hauntings within this great state. However, as these legends and stories have been passed down through sometimes many generations, and also with the certainty that these same stories have been told time and again, I decided to choose the less publicized stories of hauntings and ghostly encounters to fill the pages of this book. In fact, these lesser known stories seem to offer a bit more in the way of personal and truly mind altering material than the well known legends that others have documented.

As I spoke with various individuals concerning their ghostly contacts, I immediately noticed that the truly personal encounters with spirits of the dead spoke volumes. These encounters were not only fresh in the minds of those that have experienced these mysterious visitations, but also being that these encounters happened to individuals not inviting the paranormal to enter their lives, the report of each encounter seemed to increase in intensity. Oftentimes, the "famous" ghostly encounters that one reads about lack this intensity as the true material associated with the encounter has been lost with the telling of the tale sometimes hundreds of times.

As I listened to the residents of Pennsylvania explain their ghostly happenings, I found that, on occasion, what each frightened individual had encountered was not a ghost in the true sense of the word. On occasion, individuals encounter something other than dear departed friends or loved ones attempting the make contact from the other side. On occasion, as I studied the many types of paranormal happenings that presented themselves to numerous individuals, I found that a certain percentage of visitations sounded remarkably similar to encounters with God's heavenly helpers. Angelic encounters sometimes resemble ghostly encounters in that they both have a ""spiritual origin" or "spiritual feel" to them. However, ghostly beings that choose to make their presence known were once inhabitants of the earth that were, at one time counted among the living. Angelic beings, on the other hand, are God's helpers to all of humanity in times of need and possess a heavenly origin.

On other occasions, people believing that they had experienced an encounter with a once living spirit have actually encountered something of total and undeniable evil. As I listened to a famous, syndicated talk show that deals with several types of paranormal topics, I was surprised to find that many stories that were told of ghostly encounters were actually visits from negative spirits that never physically walked the face of the earth.

Ghosts! of Pennsylvania

As you read this book consisting of a compilation of truly bizarre happenings with ghosts, certain names and places have been obscured to protect not only the identity of the person, or persons, involved in the encounter but also, in certain instances, the area of the alleged visitation. Oftentimes, when I was asked to obscure the area of the state where an encounter allegedly occurred, I attempted to name an area that was very close in proximity to the actual encounter to show the general area of the contact. Also, as I currently have two other books on the market that deal with the paranormal happenings that consistently present themselves on the battlefield at Gettysburg, I couldn't resist the temptation to include a few stories that deal with that famous area of the state.

As with all documented ghost sightings, I cannot claim that all of the stories contained within this book are true. In fact, there is not an author today that can, without a doubt, state that every story that appears in their pages can be proven or disproved as the ghostly realm is truly an elusive subject to write about.

However, I trust that you will enjoy reading the material presented in this book as much as I have enjoyed investigating and writing about this same material. So, without further delay, I present to you, "Ghosts of Pennsylvania!"

Snow-Blind

(Gettysburg, Pennsylvania)

The weather around Devil's Den on the battlefield at Gettysburg had become something resembling an arctic winter. This change in climate, however, wasn't a surprise to the residents of this Civil War town as it was forecast many days previous to this one that the harsh northern winds would descend on the area. With the winds beginning to howl and a harsh sleet pounding the whole area in and around Devil's Den, with the sleet forecast to eventually change to snow, a solitary living soul braves these harsh elements and walks the battlefield.

This mid-January day had begun unseasonably warm for this area of the country. The solitary soul that would brave these elements did so at his own risk. George White had always wanted to visit the Gettysburg Battlefield but, living in the distant state of Alabama, he hadn't the chance to frequent the area due to the distance between his residence and the battlefield. This day however, as luck would have it, he was traveling through the area on business, business that would eventually take him to the Harrisburg area. And, as he wasn't scheduled for his business meeting until the next day, he decided to spend the day on the battlefield, even though the weather reports were all pointing to a massive cold front that would be entering the area this day.

As the day began for this southerner, he walked the town of Gettysburg and viewed many historical buildings that he had read about in the many Civil War books that he owned. After his jaunt through the main part of town, George decided to park his vehicle and walk down Steinwehr Avenue to see what the many shops in this area of town had to offer. After purchasing a battlefield map at one of the establishments, he decided that it was now time for him to take a self-guided tour of this great battlefield.

After viewing many areas of the battlefield, George parked his car at the small parking lot directly in front of the mass of boulders that make up Devil's Den. As he exited his vehicle, he noticed an abrupt change in the weather with colder winds beginning to make their presence known than he had previously experienced. Also, he couldn't help but notice the small blankets of sleet beginning to bounce off of everything in the area in which he now stood. However, this man from Alabama decided that, despite the ominous weather reports, he would brave the elements and continue on with his sight seeing adventure. After all, he reasoned, this might be the only chance that he will ever have to take in the sights and sounds of the Gettysburg Battlefield.

After viewing Devil's Den and the Triangular Field, situated very close behind Devil's Den, he began to walk back to his car. After he had reached his car, he couldn't help but notice a small building directly across from a very small bridge that spans the width of the small stream known

10

as Plum Run. After walking the short distance to the small building, he was disappointed to find that the structure was only a restroom for visitors to the battlefield. However, as he looked around the small building, he was pleased to find two paths that led into the woods. Not knowing where either of these paths would lead, George decided to take the path that led up a hill to the left of the restroom.

As he walked, the sleet coming down became almost unbearable to him as he pulled a scarf around his face. Immediately thinking that this excursion might have to end very soon due to the inclement weather, George stopped and looked around the densely wooded area that he was now in the middle of. Looking to his left, he thought that he viewed a small monument through the terrible ice falling from the heavens above. So, without delay, George walked the short distance to the monument to not only view the memorial but also to hide behind the man-made shield to deflect the falling ice and the fierce winter wind. As he crouched behind the monument, he noticed that the ice falling from the sky was very quickly turning into a massive snowstorm, a snowstorm the magnitude that he had never before experienced before in the south. Peering around the corner of the statue, George became slightly alarmed when he thought that he was now viewing another person in the distance through the heavy snow. As he stared at the figure through the storm, it appeared to him to be a Civil War reenactor also caught in what was fast becoming the storm of the century. After wiping his eyes of the falling snow, George heard the reenactor speak in a serious tone. As George continued viewing the man, the reenactor sternly

11

yelled at George to leave the area. Then, the figure pointed in the direction of George's car. As a very heavy squall of snow and wind seemed headed his way, George again ducked behind the lifesaver of a monument for a moment. After the squall had passed, George again looked around the monument in which he was against and found, to his surprise, the reenactor that he had viewed only moments before had disappeared! But, how could this have happened, as it was only a matter of seconds since he had taken his eyes off of the man in the distance?

Braving the elements, George walked the short distance to where he had seen the reenactor a short time before. As he pulled his coat around his body ever tighter, he reached the area in question. However, as he viewed the entire area, he did not find a trace of the man that he had seen only moments before! Also, even more alarming to him, there were no footprints in the snow where the reenactor was observed!

With the sighting of what George thought was an ancient Civil War spirit, along with the increasingly violent snowstorm, George decided that he had had enough of the Gettysburg Battlefield and ran back to his waiting auto. As he reached safety in the town of Gettysburg, he entered an establishment to partake of some alcoholic refreshment to hopefully calm his nerves.

As he sat in the building with no patrons inside the structure on this terribly cold and blustery winter's day, the owner of the bar noticed that George appeared a bit nervous. After asking George if he could be of assistance, George told of his ghostly encounter out on the snowy battlefield. Not knowing the ghostly history of the battlefield, George was taken by surprise when the owner of the establishment informed him that "This kind of thing happens all the time. Some of these dead soldiers just refuse to rest, I guess."

After his drink, George White entered his car and traveled the snow-covered highways to Harrisburg to find a nice, safe motel away from the town of Gettysburg. George reasoned that, even though the drive to Harrisburg on snow-covered roads could be hazardous, staying in a motel near a haunted piece of Pennsylvania real estate could be even more hazardous, hazardous to the mind of this one time non-believer in the paranormal!

Devil's Den. The point of origin of the ghostly walk.

Guardian From The Past

(Altoona, Pennsylvania)

Sabrina Bonner jumped for joy as she ran through what was to become her very first home away from her family. As a new graduate from a small college in Ohio, Sabrina had just migrated east to the outskirts of Altoona, Pennsylvania to begin a job that she was recently hired for and to search for a home in which to live. After a moderate amount of travel throughout the area, Sabrina found a very small "bungalow" that was, as luck would have it, for sale. Upon entering the property she noticed that the small home was in very good condition with a neatly manicured, although very small, front yard. A small area for a garden was located behind the home.

After a minimal amount of thought, Sabrina decided that she would dial the realtor's phone number that was on the for-sale sign in front of the home and inquire about this positively lovely house. After consulting the realtor and inquiring about the cost of the home, Sabrina was overjoyed that her dream home was well within her budget. While hanging up the phone, Sabrina displayed an ever-widening smile at the prospect of owning this dream home.

So, without further delay, she again contacted the realtor and made plans to secure a loan to obtain what was to become her beautiful new dwelling.

After moving into her new residence, she found items from the previous owner still in the attic, covered with a small coating of dust. A very small, cramped attic with little light was something that, as a child, used to frighten her so, she abruptly exited the cramped confines of the dusty attic and proceeded to the main area of the house. As she hurried to return to the main area of the house, she wondered who the previous owner of this gorgeous home could have been. Whoever the previous owner was, it was obvious to Sabrina that he or she had taken very good care of the structure, as very little work was necessary for her to undertake before the residence was completely to her liking.

Several days after Sabrina had finished with everything that needed to be accomplished for her successful move, she sat at the lone window at the rear of her home and looked into the thickly grown woods that surrounded her humble little abode. Thinking that this was the perfect scene for a woodland walk, Sabrina slipped on her shoes and walked the very short distance to the wooded area behind her home. As she walked, Sabrina was surprised at how undisturbed the land around her home was. After all, Sabrina had no neighbors for nearly one mile from her home; her only friends would be the abundant wildlife that ran through the woods and across her small yard.

As she re-entered her home, she noticed a chill in the air that wasn't present when she began her little excursion. As

Ghosts! of Pennsylvania

fall was quickly turning into the long months of winter, she realized that a drastic change in the weather could happen in this central Pennsylvania land at any time. As Sabrina entered her home, she slipped off her shoes and began to prepare a cup of tea for herself. She then sat down on her favorite chair in the living room and relaxed while darkness enveloped the property around her home. After sitting with her eyes closed for quite some time, she became startled when, after re-opening her eyes, she thought that she had caught a glimpse of a person disappear into the hallway that led to the staircase. Blinking her eyes several times in disbelief, she reasoned that a person could not have entered her home in the time that she rested, as she hadn't heard anything enter her home while she sat.

Still, her curiosity got the best of her as she rose from her chair and walked the short distance to where she thought she saw the dark figure walk. Peering around the corner and now viewing the dark and lonely staircase, she saw nothing, but immediately thought of the previous owner's possessions in her attic. Attempting to clear her mind of such curious thoughts, Sabrina decided to take a shower and then sleep the night away as the late fall winds howled around her small home.

The next day, Sabrina arose to a dark late-fall sky and colder than normal temperatures. After a quick cup of coffee, Sabrina again thought of the contents of her attic. Wishing to satisfy her curiosity, she walked the short distance to the upstairs room that contained the stairs that led to her attic. Holding a small flashlight, Sabrina breathed a forceful breath and proceeded to enter the main area of the cramped room above her home. Articles of old clothing took up most of the contents of her attic. Ancient clothes from a time gone by met her eyes. Suddenly, Sabrina's thoughts were interrupted by a faint knock at her living-room door. Only too happy to exit the gloomy attic, Sabrina ran down the two flights of stairs and opened the door that led to her front yard. Standing before her was a very old lady, nicely dressed and smiling. In her right hand she held a small cake wrapped in brown paper.

Startled by the appearance of the old woman standing at her door, Sabrina gasped and uttered a somewhat nervous "hello." The old woman said nothing. She simply held out her right hand to offer the small cake to Sabrina. Accepting the gift, Sabrina asked the old lady if she would like to come in and warm herself before proceeding back to…wherever she had come from. The old lady smiled at Sabrina and said "I must return to my own. Perhaps another time, my dear. Perhaps another time." She then abruptly turned and began to walk very quickly away from Sabrina's home. Now filled with wonder, Sabrina called to the little old lady, "Who are you? Where did you come from?" The old lady didn't break stride and didn't turn to speak. However, she did utter what Sabrina thought was a very strange answer to her questions. Without skipping a beat, the old lady yelled, with her back turned to Sabrina, "I'm Mrs. Singerham. I'm from somewhere that only I know and that you will someday be."

Immediately shutting the door with a force that she didn't think she could muster, Sabrina held her back against the inside of her front door and shut her eyes. Wondering who this very strange old lady could be, she ran to the nearest window and peaked through a small crack in the curtain. The little lady was no where in sight. Sabrina reasoned that, as she slammed the door and waited, the little old lady must've escaped in the dense forest that engulfed her home.

Now, taking a deep breath, Sabrina suddenly remembered the small cake that the old lady had offered her as a gift. She must have dropped it in all of the confusion, as she became frightened at the weird answers to her questions that the old lady offered. However, as she traced the few steps that led to her front door, the small wrapped gift was no where to be found.

Thinking that she must have imagined the whole episode, Sabrina changed her clothes and decided that she would travel the short distance to the town of Altoona and have breakfast at a diner. While at the diner, Sabrina struck up a conversation with several people. As she was new in town, the older people in the diner attempted to make her feel at home and welcomed her to their area of the country. Telling all at the diner that she had just bought the little home only a short distance up the road from the east end of the town, an old gent leaned around and said that he hoped that she would not only enjoy her new home but also the entire town of Altoona as well. With a smile, Sabrina thanked the kindly gent and offered her hand as a sign of friendship and gratitude. As the old gentleman shook Sabrina's hand, he exclaimed, "If she were alive today, I'm sure that old Mrs. Singerham would love to have seen you in what was her beloved home."

Shock entered the entire being of Sabrina as she gasped at what was just said by the old man. Mrs. Singerham had indeed welcomed young Sabrina to her humble abode. Only, this welcome came from a world that only Mrs. Singerham knows!!

Cadence Of Time

(Gettysburg, Pennsylvania)

What inspires people to visit here? What are the reasons that some individuals come to this place on a consistent basis, never having enough of the history that reaches out, much as a spirit reaches for the everlasting life in Heaven? The beauty of the battlefield and the history of this place certainly add to the reasons that so many visit these hallowed grounds every year.

One of the most visited and studied areas of this great battlefield is the area known as Pickett's Charge, an area where a multitude of brave Southern souls prepared to meet their maker after their failed attack on the Union line that held strong on Cemetery Ridge. Many are the sounds that one hears during a summer day in this area of the battlefield. From tour buses moving down Confederate Avenue to the sound of children playing in the open field that saw so much death and destruction in July of 1863.

However, when night falls, and if you are one of the "lucky" individuals to witness the soldiers that died so long ago in this field of battle, your senses might become mesmerized with wonder and anxiety. Or, the truly unique individual will welcome the battlefield dead in whatever form they choose to enter this dimension.

Ghosts! of Pennsylvania

For Kristin Anne Johnson and her friend Carla, the
moment that was about to unfold before their very eyes
became the highlight of their most recent trip to these
haunted grounds of history.

Their frightening episode began with a visit to the area
of the battlefield that displays an obviously gallant
Confederate General riding a brilliant steed atop an expertly
forged marble base. The Virginia monument with
Confederate General Robert E. Lee atop his horse Traveler
overlooks the area where many Confederate soldiers
began their assault on the Union lines approximately one
mile in the distance. This was the starting point for Kristin
and her friend as they decided to travel, on foot, the same
area where so many souls began their ascent into eternity
so many years ago.

As the two friends walked a few feet from their vehicle to
begin their modern-day assault on the area of Cemetery
Ridge, nothing out of the ordinary was sensed by these two
Civil War buffs. However, as they continued their march on
the field of death, 100 yards from their point of origin, Kristin
stopped dead in her tracks and listened. Carla, noticing
that her friend was not by her side, turned and asked Kristin
why she had stopped their march to glory. Kristin
immediately related that she had heard a voice calling in
the distance. However, this voice sounded remarkably like
the voice of an Indian and not a voice of the typical visitor
to the battlefield. Kristin had ceased her walking and had
turned with full expectation to see a Native American
standing in the distance. However, as her eyes scanned the

land behind her, this now bewildered visitor saw not a living soul. After this strange incident, both women again began their walk in the open field before them. As they walked, another unexplainable occurrence presented itself. What sounded to Carla like an eerie drum cadence coming from a totally enclosed room in the distance filled Kristin's friend's ears. However, as the field of Pickett's Charge is very wide open and spacious, a sound that flowed across this field should have sounded much different than the one that was displayed for Carla to hear. Kristin, standing only mere feet from her friend, could not hear the sound of a distant drum.

However, as she walked the short distance to where Carla was standing, she too began hearing the eerie sound that came from an unseen area. However, as each friend spoke of what they were experiencing, it became clear to each of them that the drum cadence that each girl heard was totally different! Each of the two bewildered visitors to this haunted battlefield experienced the sound of a lone drum beat. However, each drum cadence that each heard was of a totally different rhythm!

When asked what she thought each cadence might have represented, Kristin stated, "Anyone that studies the Civil War will remember that the corps, regiments and battalions marching together, sometimes used different bugle calls and drum cadences for their troops so that each man knew what maneuver he was supposed to execute." Based on this statement, Kristin feels very strongly that what she, as well as her friend, heard on that day was a sound a differing drum cadences from the past, beats that filtered down through the centuries for each of them to experience.

As both Kristin and Carla stood very still and listened to the strange sounds from a time long since departed into the annals of history, the intensity of excitement began to enable them to overcome their fears. Were they truly hearing something from the actual battle played out so many seasons ago?

As they continued their walk, the sound of drums began to fade away in the field of battle for these two appreciative Civil War buffs. As they reached their destination on the battlefield, both Kristin and Carla were silent. In their minds, they thought, in silent reverence, of the men who had courageously laid down their lives for what they believed.

Then, as the silence of contemplation became shattered, the sound of cannons firing from somewhere on the field of battle pierced the still air. As this unnatural sound filled their ears, each girl looked at the other in amazement. Attempting to rationalize what the sounds of the ghostly cannonading might be, they reasoned that, as there were no reenactments taking place and no tourists or tour buses anywhere in the area, what they were hearing must again be something not of this world. They felt that they were again experiencing another sound of war, compliments of the long dead Gettysburg combatants that selflessly laid down their lives so many decades ago.

After hearing this sound from the past, the women decided to retrace their steps across the field of Pickett's Charge and return to their waiting automobile. However, as they neared their car, Carla immediately stopped. When

Ghosts! of Pennsylvania

Kristin turned to look at Carla, she couldn't help but notice the peculiar expression etched on her face. Kristin then asked Carla what was wrong and had she again experienced something out of the ordinary? Carla immediately said to her friend, "You were right. There must've been Indians here! I can hear them yelling!" However, these were not the strange sounds of Indian calls floating down through the ages for the girls to experience. These were the sounds of the famous "Rebel Yell" that was used by the Confederate Army before each attack. As the two were very near what was the Confederate lines on that day, the familiar sound of the Confederates beginning their march with the accustomed yell filled the girls' ears.

In closing, Kristin offers the following. "For those to whom we have told this story to and said they still don't believe in ghosts, let me just say this. I respect all for which these men died. Whether they were from the North or the South, they had the belief that what they were fighting for was the right cause. And the brief moment in time that I spent, along with Carla, on this glorious, hallowed ground, I felt as if these men opened a door so that I may truly understand the history of what took place in this small Pennsylvania town.

"If you happen to go to Gettysburg for a history lesson. You may just get what you came for. I encourage you to listen to these spirits with all your five senses. It is the spirits of these men who have been my greatest history teachers!"

Area of the Gettysburg Battlefield
Where ghostly drums were heard.

Farewell Encounter

(Tyrone, Pennsylvania)

They had been married for what seemed an eternity. After their marriage in 1931, two children and many grandchildren became the pride and joy of this elderly couple. Through the years they had seen the good and bad, hard times as well as good and prosperous times. The hard times, however, seemed only to strengthen the intense bond that each of them had for each other. As this very grateful and blessed couple grew older, the usual dose of illness set in, mostly for the gentleman. After many years of blissful marriage, Mr. Foreman suffered a heart attack that seemed to set him back, health-wise, a number of years. However, with his faithful wife by his side, Joe Foreman recuperated due not only to the health-care professionals that tended to his every need, but also because of his loving wife, Virginia, that catered to her beloved in his time of need.

Six months after Joe Foreman's heart-attack, his wife became very ill with a sickness that left her very weak and often unable to even walk the short distance to their kitchen. Much as Virginia Foreman had cared for her loving husband, Joe Foreman also spent long hours with his wife, hoping and praying that God wouldn't take her just yet.

Ghosts! of Pennsylvania

However, after a lengthy illness, Virginia Foreman was taken to her Heavenly Reward in the hands of her Guardian Angel.

Her husband Joe was completely devastated by the loss of his life-long spouse. After the usual condolences that were paid by various family members and friends, Joe settled into what was now his lonely home and thought of the many memories that he and Virginia had been blessed with. As Joe began to cry uncontrollably as he thought of his deceased wife, he thought that he heard Virginia's voice call out to him. Looking all around the room that he was sitting in, Joe didn't view anything unusual and thought that his grief was beyond what he was used to facing and that he was now rationalizing that his deceased wife might still be with him.

However, as Joe closed his eyes to rest his weary mind, he again heard the voice of Virginia calling to him from what sounded like the kitchen area of his home. Now, completely sure that he had heard a loving voice calling out to him, Joe immediately rose from his easy chair and walked very quickly into his kitchen. When he reached the area where he thought he had heard his wife's voice, he was disappointed to find nothing in the immediate area. However, as Joe was about to leave the kitchen, he felt the urge to look out the kitchen window that led to a view of the back yard. There, standing only mere feet from the window, was Virginia! A white translucent gown flowing in the breeze wrapped around her immaculate body. The wide smile that was etched on the ghostly apparition's face told Joe all that he needed to know concerning the happiness that Virginia

27

was experiencing. Then, after what seemed to be a very short time, the apparition of Virginia was gone.

Joe could hardly believe that he had seen his wife one last time as a ghostly apparition behind his home. Joe again began to cry; however, this time, the tears were not all grief-induced. Now, a certain amount of happiness blended in with his sadness as Joe's feelings became mixed.

Had Joe Foreman really viewed an apparition of his recently deceased wife? Various reports that have circulated throughout the years claim that if a person is grieving beyond what that person is physically capable of enduring, God will allow one final visit from the deceased to comfort the person that is in intense pain and sorrow. Joe was sure that he had had a visit from his lovely wife after she had physically departed from this earth.

Not long after Joe viewed his loving wife, he too departed this earth to be with his beloved Virginia. Now, all grieving is complete. Life in Heaven has come to this most deserving couple.

Where The Dead Walk

(Ramey, Pennsylvania)

It stands high on a hill and, by its outward appearance, gives all that gaze upon it a feeling of evil, a feeling that something just might live behind its dark walls. The house has been vacant for as long as people of the town of Ramey, Pennsylvania can remember. Although showing obvious signs of age, the structure is still very sturdy and, if one would be willing to undertake the operation, could be renovated for future use.

The home, however, has been dubbed as being haunted by some in the community and, for this reason, finds no buyers to take over its occupancy. Many of the children that go to school in the area speak of lurid tales of spirits of the evil dead roaming the halls and the upstairs rooms at night. This, however, must simply be the childrens' wild and vivid imaginations as no firm evidence has ever been found to substantiate such a claim. However, no one dares enter the dark and overgrown area that the ominous looking house sits on. By its outward appearance, it truly does appear that something not of this world could inhabit the eerie structure. With broken windows, slamming shutters and doors that are gone from the structure, the home does give all appearances of a ghostly residence.

Ghosts! of Pennsylvania

A small group of high school classmates congregate in a classroom study hall. The conversation of this small group of boys turns to the house that is purportedly haunted in the Ramey area. Stating that no one has ever entered the house to check on the claim of its haunted nature, one particularly brave individual boldly states that he wouldn't mind spending a night in the house but only if someone would accompany him to the area. As the other boys laugh at this "brave" individual that needs accompaniment to the home, two others offer that, if they can sneak away from their parents, they would also accompany the boy in his adventure into the purportedly haunted structure. After all, how haunted can the place be as there hasn't really been an actual sighting of a ghost there.

When the school day ends, the three boys that are going to tempt fate and stay in the house on the hill meet outside their school. They all agree that this Friday night they will meet outside the home at 8 PM and begin their adventure.

As Friday evening unfolds, only two of the three brave souls show up for their night in the haunted residence. Assuming that the other boy has "chickened out" for fear of the unknown, the other two boys enter the house through the front door that has been gone from the home for quite some time. Shining a flashlight around the downstairs rooms, each boy now experiences the rush of fear as blood pressures begin to rise, although each boy will not admit their fear.

As the boys climb the dark and gloomy staircase to reach the upper rooms, a soft moan is heard from above them. Immediately stopping in their tracks on the staircase,

Ghosts! *of Pennsylvania*

one of the boys reason that what they had just heard
must've been the wind whistling through the open windows
of the upstairs rooms. Immediately agreeing with his friend,
the two boys press on to their ultimate destination.

When they reach the top of the staircase, the boys see
nothing but three empty rooms that were obviously once
used for bedrooms. Breathing a sigh of relief, the boys
descend the staircase and light the small kerosene lantern
that they had brought with them. As they sit in what was the
living room of the vacant house, they tell of the many
stories that each has heard over the years concerning the
house. One boy claims that a wicked man who had
practiced witchcraft owned the home. The other boy, not to
be outdone, states that he heard a family was murdered in
the very room in which they now sit and that the bodies of
the victims were buried in the cellar.

Many more stories flow from the mouths of the two boys
as darkness of the night fills the eerie structure that will not
be vacant this night. The room in which the boys sit was
very dark as they entered but, as it is now very close to 11
PM, the home is now totally engulfed in complete darkness.

Being that it is now quite late, the two brave souls decide
to unroll their sleeping bags and attempt to get some sleep.
After all, the more they sleep, the less they will have to think
about what might happen in this haunted mansion. And,
when the sun rises, the two extremely brave young men will
be the talk of their classmates at school.

As each boy falls into a deep sleep, neither is aware that
something has awoken in the upstairs rooms. However,
after only a short time, each boy is stirred by ominous

31

sounds from one of the upper rooms! With each boy looking at each other in disbelief, one of the two boys whisper that the house really IS haunted after all as evidence by the sounds from above their heads. As the boys sit up in fear that seems to paralyze them, the distinct sound of very heavy footsteps from someone obviously large in stature enters the hallway that leads to the staircase! As this unknown person or spirit begins his descent to the  floor in which the boys sit, the two boys immediately run to the front doorway and out into the night. As one of the boys glances back to the opening that once held the front door of the house, he thinks that he observes the outline of a man reaching out to the running lads. Quickly turning his head so he wouldn't have to view this dreadful sight, the two boys run to the main part of town and collapse on the sidewalk in exhaustion.

As both boys catch their breath, each talks hysterically about what they had just encountered. The old dilapidated house on the edge of town IS haunted. Now, when they hear a story being offered concerning the haunted house, each boy will not only agree with what they hear but will inform the teller of the ghost story of their first-hand account with the specter that beckoned them to return to his ghostly abode.

Ghostly Assistance?

(Indiana, Altoona, Pennsylvania)

A thoroughly terrified young man crawls along a deserted and snow covered route 422 near Indiana, Pennsylvania in his small Chevy automobile in the dead of winter. All that this person sees around him just east of Indiana is whiteout conditions brought on by a very heavy snowfall. One and one half feet of the fluffy white precipitation has fallen and has forced the State of Pennsylvania to close the road that this individual now travels on. As it is now late afternoon, the man in the auto begins to feel the presence of snow-blindness entering his mind as the light of day begins to dim. With a moderate snow still falling and snow all around him as far as his tired eyes can see, he begins to panic. Would his vehicle end up like the multitude of disabled cars and 18-wheelers that are abandoned by the roadside that he now travels on?

As he wonders how he entered into this mess, he immediately sees a weird presence in the sky in the form of a glowing light. The strange blue light takes on an indiscernible shape and then disappears in an instant. Thinking that his mind is now thoroughly confused with fright and intense feelings of dread, the young man in a potentially fateful situation continues on his way. If his car

33

would stop at any time in the deep snow, he would most definitely be stranded for perhaps several days in the frigid temperatures and barren wasteland of snow and ice. Timothy Johns had just graduated from Mount Aloysius College in the spring of 1992. His field of study would take him into various fieldwork sites across the State of Pennsylvania before he would be eligible for certification in his chosen field. His first fieldwork location in Clarion, Pennsylvania had been a most pleasant experience. However, his recent travels to complete his fieldwork in Butler, Pennsylvania had been trying at best. Traveling to Butler, PA in the dead of winter each week had been very stressful for the young man. However, nothing could have prepared him for this Arctic blast that mercilessly hit central Pennsylvania with full force.

As Timothy was preparing to leave his assignment in Butler for his home in Altoona, PA one Friday afternoon, his room-mate warned him that he had recently received word from his mother that all of the roads in the central Pennsylvania region were closed due to a massive snowstorm that blanketed the area. Not being able to accept being cooped up in a small dormitory for the weekend, Timothy decided to tempt fate and travel the three hours it would take him to reach his destination. After all, how much snow could there be in his hometown of Altoona as there was only a small coating of the fluffy white flakes in Butler as he entered his waiting automobile?

As he traveled, the snow indeed became heavier and the clouds more ominous as he ventured further away from his fieldwork site. As he entered Indiana, Pennsylvania he encountered his worst fears as his small car barely crept along in the deepening snow. Thinking that he should possibly find a motel in the area and let the snowstorm pass, he immediately thought of his home and how he would miss seeing his parents. So, with fear in his heart and mind, he entered the outskirts of Indiana and trudged on in the worsening snowstorm.

Now very close to his home, Timothy still continues to wonder about the very strange glow that he had seen in the snowy sky several miles back on route 422. Was this eerie glow some sort of sign that he should not go on but turn and spend the night in a safe place? Or, was the glow that he had seen some ghostly passenger that returns to the area to warn drivers of impending doom when violent or unsafe weather is about to take place?

The only thing that Timothy knew as he slowly made his way along the icy roads of Altoona was that his trip had taken him much longer than he had anticipated. The normal time that a trip from his fieldwork site in Butler to his home on the outskirts of Altoona should take would be approximately 3 hours. This trip, however, took him 5 hours and has seemed to take the life out of this nervous young man.

As he pulls into his parents' driveway, he breaths a sigh of relief to have been able to travel treacherous roads that seemingly no one else had the ability to travel on. As he exits his snow-covered vehicle, Timothy hears a sound that he will never forget considering the circumstances that he might have been put into on his long and grueling trip. The left rear tire of his car is shredded beyond recognition! What little air had been in the tire was now leaking into nothingness. Knowing that he shouldn't have been able to travel on a tire so mangled beyond recognition with the steel belts of the tire coming out of the tire at all angles, Timothy thinks back to the weird light in the sky that had disappeared as his fears intensified on his journey home. Was this glow that he had experienced two hours before pulling into his driveway a ghost or something more? Was an angel watching over Timothy as he ventured through extremely difficult territory? Either ghostly helper or angelic helper, Timothy doesn't care. All he knows is that he should not have made it home on three tires without the help of something or someone as he traveled on what should have been impassable roads.

Phantom Sounds Of The Battlefield

(Gettysburg, Pennsylvania)

Tho drums of the Confederacy as well as the Union have been silent for many decades. With the formal treaty of surrender signed by Confederate Commander Robert E. Lee at Appomattox Courthouse after years of bloodshed in the 1860's, the Civil War came to an agonizing close. The remaining survivors of this famous clash then went their separate ways and back to their homes to begin life anew.

However, it has been stated many times that the men that died in the battles for Union as well as Confederate territories still linger on the place where they fell so many seasons ago. Many recent documentations of the Civil War dead arising at the battlefield at Gettysburg attest to the fact that something not of this world continually rises from the terrain at Gettysburg. The phenomenon of ghostly encounters on the Gettysburg battlefield, though only recently documented, began many years ago with encounters from the Civil War dead probably going back as far as the actual battle itself.

In the 1960's, the battlefield at Gettysburg looked much different than the present-day Military Park. However, the

37

same spirits that attempted to make their presence known in that decade continue this day to reach out to many that frequent this area of bloodshed.

Some time ago, I was contacted by a person not of this country concerning his terrifying experience at Gettysburg. The person that made contact with me via e-mail resides in the country of Slovakia. While Slovakia has also seen its share of bloodshed, the American Civil War is little known by most habitants of that country. However, as the person in question was originally from the United States, he shared an incident with me that happened to him when he was still living in this country.

Sam Hacking was in his teenage years when he visited the Gettysburg Battlefield in the 1960's. In fact, Sam and his family attempted to make yearly trips to the battlefield during this time-frame. On his very first visit to the battlefield, Sam inadvertently became immersed in the haunting activity that plays out on the battlefield at Gettysburg on a regular basis.

Sam and his family had arrived in Gettysburg and settled into what was to be their motel for the night. However, as there was still much sunlight left in the day, Sam and his family decided to tour the battlefield for the very first time. The next day, as it was pre-planned, Sam and his family would be experiencing a very long tour on the battlefield, compliments of one of the licensed tour guides.

After their rather brief trip in and around the battlefield, Sam and his family made the very short journey back to their motel. The motel was situated very close to the main part of the Gettysburg Battlefield. As Sam and his family had decided to rise very early the next morning to begin their long tour of the battlefield, Sam decided to attempt to fall asleep somewhat early in the evening to be totally refreshed for the big excursion planned for the following day. However, after quite some time of not being able to sleep, Sam experienced what he believes to have been a very real encounter with the ghosts at Gettysburg.

While he lay in bed, Sam heard the continual sound of a drum-roll being played out on the darkened fields of battle. Even at the age of 13 or 14, he ruled out all possible "natural" sounds and continued listening intently at the ghostly drums of a by-gone era. Since it was extremely dark out on the battlefield with no reenactors in sight, Sam concluded that what he was experiencing until he drifted off to sleep was sounds from the past, the sounds of ghostly rhythm kept by a soul long since departed from this world.

As there are many accounts of ghostly sounds being experienced out on the battlefield at Gettysburg after the sun falls in the west, this experience by young Sam Hacking isn't uncommon to the area. However, when one is in the process of experiencing something that shouldn't be happening, the mind will hold on to the memory of the encounter with the dead for a lifetime.

In his correspondence to me, Sam closes his letter by saying, "I know that I will always have this memory of Gettysburg and yes, I believe that the horror of those three days (of relentless fighting on July 1,2,3 of 1863) was powerful enough in its shock-filled energy to permanently lock all of those souls, sights and sounds on the spot where they are perceived by the living even today."

Artifacts from the Battle of Gettysburg.
Could this be the ghostly drum
from ages past?

Ghostly Flight

(Rural central Pennsylvania)

A middle aged man steers his ATV (all-terrain vehicle) up a long and winding dirt road behind his home. On many Sunday evenings in the spring and summer, Johnathan Shorter travels the short distance from his home to a most secluded area. This is his private, little getaway from family and friends.

This area that Johnathan enjoys on most Sunday evenings was at one time the area of a coal-stripping job. Located on top of a large hill with trees cleared for approximately one-half square mile, this is the perfect setting for stargazing on moonlit summer nights. Johnathan parks his ATV at a spot very familiar to him and leans back to enjoy the beauty of the summer night. The only company that he will have on most nights is the woodland creatures that graze the land around him and the occasional shooting star. However, on this night, Johnathan will witness something very different and frightening as he stares into the heavens.

As he leans back and looks at the beautiful summer sky, Johnathan views a jet flying overhead. Normally, this is a common sight at his little hideaway in the wilderness. This jet, however, seems somewhat different than anything he has seen before. As he looks up into the open sky, Johnathan notices that this jet appears to have an eerie glow completely surrounding it! Thinking that this jet might be experiencing some mechanical problems, he listens for the sound of the massive engines that he normally hears as each jet passes in the night. However, not a sound is heard from up above.

Suddenly, something catches Johnathan's attention at the edge of the woods, merely one quarter of a mile away from him. Not believing in ghosts or hauntings, Johnathan tries to explain away what he is now witnessing a short distance from his parked ATV. Johnathan is now witnessing what appear to be several people walking, or floating at the edge of the woods. Normally, this would not be a cause for alarm; however, these people too appear to be giving off a light unto themselves.

After a quick glance into the sky, the luminous jet is now nowhere to be seen, Johnathan now starts his ATV and rides very quickly to his home one mile away from his present position. As he enters his home, he explains his adventure to his wife, who reassures him that he must have imagined the whole episode.

After much thought and conversation with his wife, Johnathan agrees that he must have imagined the whole scenario as, his wife reasons, there is really no such thing as a ghost.

After a brief time conversing with his wife, Johnathan decides to slip into bed and rest for his day of work the following morning. However, as he sleeps, Johnathan experiences the most vivid of dreams. A jet, much like the one that he had seen on his woodland excursion, loses altitude and crashes in a densely wooded area of the country. All aboard are seemingly killed from the extremely violent impact. However, shortly after this nightmare, another begins as Johnathan dreams that several of the passengers on board the crashed jet are now in his room encircling his very bed! The same glow that he had seen in the woods is now enveloping each dead individual.

Abruptly waking in a cold sweat, Johnathan cannot believe that the nightmare he had experienced only moments before had seemed so real and the bodies around his bed so lifelike. Lying back down on his bed, he stares at the ceiling and wishes that morning would come so that he could be bathed in the sunlight of a new day.

Finally, after what seems to him like many hours, the morning sun begins its ascent in the east and Johnathan rises from his bed and begins his morning routine. As he pours a cup of coffee into his coffee mug, he switches on his radio to catch the morning news before he takes a shower and heads out the door for a day of work. However, as he listens to the radio, he is met with a report that reaches his very soul. Dropping his coffee mug on the kitchen floor, Johnathan listens as the announcer leads his top stories of the day with a plane crash in rural Pennsylvania that claimed the lives of all passengers on board the ill-fated flight. The time of the crash? The exact time that Johnathan woke from his very life-like nightmare!

Had Johnathan Shorter viewed a plane flying over his area of relaxation in the woods that was doomed to death for all on board? One never knows the power of the human mind and the God-given gift of certain people with ESP (extra-sensory perception). Johnathan, however, prays that this gift does not become a common occurrence in his life. At least not for viewing something so heart-wrenching and life-altering.

Inquisitive Soul
(Clearfield, Pennsylvania)

The house located in one of the more remote areas of Clearfield, Pennsylvania had been a fixture in the area for as long as the present residents of the town could remember. To the best of anyone's knowledge, the same family had owned the moderate sized home since the structure was built in the very early 1900's. The present day appearance of the dwelling looked similar to its appearance in years past. The only noticeable change that had been made throughout the years was a fresh coat of paint on occasion.

This residence, now owned by a great-granddaughter of the original owners, has a feel of simplicity and warmth that is missing in many of the new homes of today. The lone occupant of the house, Margaret Tinsley, is a typical resident of the Clearfield area. She rises early to ready herself for her day of work and, upon completion of her day's work, returns home to live simply in the home of her ancestors. Being middle aged and single has its advantages for Margaret as she has much time to devote to cleaning and caring for her home as well as much time for her hobbies.

Ghosts! of Pennsylvania

Margaret's father had passed away of cancer in the late 90's. Her mother had not re-married and was currently a resident of a local personal care home. As Margaret had a wonderful relationship with her father and continues on with a very loving relationship with her mother, she keeps what was her parents' bedroom much as it was since her father's death. On occasion, Margaret will transport her loving mother to the home of her youth for an occasional visit. During the Christmas season, Margaret's mother again becomes a fixture within the residence until her daughter must again return her to the personal care home.

As Margaret typically has much time to devote to shopping and local travel on the weekends as well as after each workday, she oftentimes travels the short distance to the neighboring towns of Dubois or State College. On one particularly rainy night, Margaret ventured to the town of Dubois to shop in the lone mall of the area and to, afterwards, eat a mid-evening meal at one of the local restaurants. As she made her way home from her shopping excursion, she noticed that, as she traveled over Rockton Mountain, a thick fog enveloping her now slowing automobile. As she had to carefully proceed though the dangerous fog, the travel to her home in Clearfield became a much longer trip than she had anticipated. Eventually, she reached her small driveway and proceeded to the front porch of her home. However, as she approached the front porch, a vicious thunderstorm made its presence known with torrential rain, wind and lightning as Margaret scurried through the front door of her home.

Ghosts! of Pennsylvania

Now safely inside, Margaret removed her very wet coat and walked the short distance to her phone and answering machine that were situated near the staircase that led to what was once her parent's room. Seeing the blinking light on her answering machine signaling that someone had phoned while she was away, she was about to press the small button on her machine to play the recorded message when she heard a sound that made her stop and listen. The sound in question came from above her head, from what was once her parents' bedroom. As thunder clapped and the sound of rain hitting the roof of her house made her feel a bit uneasy, the sounds that emanated from above gave her the impression that a person had broken into her house while she was away and was, at the moment, walking in the upstairs bedroom and removing whatever items he or she could find. As she looked up the darkened staircase, all that Margaret could see was the outline of her parents' bedroom door as lightning illuminated the dark area of the house.

As she listened to the intruder above, Margaret wondered how an intruder could've gotten into her secure residence, as there were no signs of forced entry or other signs of intrusion by the person walking above. As Margaret listened to the sounds above her head, it was obvious to her that the intruder was acting alone as she heard the sounds of only one set of feet walking from one area of the room to the other, apparently lifting and dragging items from one area of the room to the other.

Originally thinking that she had no other option but to confront the intruder, she grabbed a steak knife from her kitchen and walked slowly and silently to the edge of the staircase. However, as fear began to grip her, she decided that she would wait for the intruder in her home's basement and meet with him or her outside after she would exit her home from a basement door.

As she sat and waited for the intruder to exit her parents' room and proceed down the staircase that led to the dining room of her home, Margaret was startled to still experience the sounds of a person walking from two floors above her. The loudness of the would-be burglar defied reason and logic and Margaret sensed that if someone were stealing items from a person's home, that person would attempt to be as quiet as possible. This person, however, was far from discreet!

After hearing the strange sounds of the person in the bedroom for over two hours, Margaret finally sensed silence in the upstairs bedroom as only a peal of thunder could be heard on occasion by this now bewildered individual. Margaret waited for quite some time and wondered why she hadn't heard the intruder leave the confines of the upstairs bedroom. Feeling a bit uneasy, Margaret nevertheless decided to attempt to sleep in the basement that night, as she did not want to travel the short distance, two floors up, to the room where the many questionable noises had occurred for the past two to three hours.

Sleep became very difficult that stormy night as Margaret sat on the lone chair that had been placed in the corner of her home's basement. However, the next morning, as she arose from a restless night's sleep, she still had visions of someone invading what was once her parents' room. As she clutched the knife that she had taken with her only hours before, she ascended the stairs from her basement. She paused and listened. No sounds could be heard from the room above. She then slowly walked to her dining room and began to climb the stairs to the bedroom. As she walked, Margaret imagined her parents' room in total disarray with many valuable items missing. However, as she entered the door that led into the room in question, Margaret was surprised to find that not one item was missing from the room and nothing had been moved from the original place in which each item sat!

As Margaret attempted to re-create the horror that she had experienced the previous night, she second-guessed her own senses and thought that maybe, in the midst of the thunderstorm, she had imagined the unmistakable sounds of a person walking and moving items within the room. However, the more she thought about this very remote possibility, she dismissed this hypothesis and searched her mind for other reasons that, at the moment, were elusive to her. After many days of thought, the only plausible explanation she could think of for the strange sounds that she had experienced only days before was that quite possibly her father, deceased for a number of years, had come back to see the room in which he had slept in so many years in the past. This, for Margaret, was the only explanation that she could think of for the truly haunting sounds that emanated from the ghostly room on that stormy night.

Even though she still had doubts as to the possible visitation she had experienced from her long dead father, all doubts were erased from her mind as she attempted to sleep in her home several nights after the frightening incident. As Margaret pulled the covers over her body and head to sleep, she almost immediately viewed a bight light in her room that lasted but a second. There, however, seemed to be no source for the strange light that filled her room. Still keeping her eyes closed and her body very still, she experienced a gentle tug on the blanket that covered her body. Now, realizing that another visitation from her deceased father might be happening at that very moment,

Margaret was surprised that she was not frightened. As she experienced these two physically impossible happenings that night, she thought back to the night, a few days before, in which she had experienced the strange sounds that filtered out of her parents' room and smiled a small smile. She now knew that the visitation she had experienced that night and the other night was a visit from her father's spirit. A spirit from beyond coming back through time to a room in which he, at one time, slept. Also, a ghostly touch on Margaret's blanket to assure his loving daughter that everything was all right in his present place of rest. This had been a surprising visit to a daughter that he once loved while on earth, a daughter that he still loves from beyond the grave.

Flashes From Beyond

(Gettysburg, Pennsylvania)

A man slowly moves across the slightly uneven terrain near the Tennessee Memorial on the battlefield at Gettysburg. The many large oak trees that offer shade to this area of the battlefield obscure the mid-day sun as the man continues what will be the walk of his life. The pleasant early fall temperatures add to the beauty of the battlefield, a battlefield with a generous amount of visitors touring the once bloody field of death. Before this man is a field that, at one time in the history of this land, became a killing field where a multitude of Confederate as well as Union soldiers breathed their last agonizing breath.

On July 3rd, 1863, the Confederate forces commanded by General Robert E. Lee marched across this open field and into the death grip that consisted of many Union soldiers and Union artillery. The survival of the Confederacy hinged on this death march into Yankee soil.

However, before this bloody march of death occurred, Confederate artillery attempted to soften the Yankee lines that existed on Cemetery Ridge with one of the most dramatic displays of bombardment in the history of man. Largely ineffective, this show of force through the massive

51

amounts of shell expended in the direction of the Union lines initiated the march that is today known as Pickett's Charge. After the cannonading had ceased, thousands of Confederate forces attempted the one mile march across the open terrain of this field and were met with a deadly barrage of gun fire that virtually destroyed the Confederate forces attempting to overthrow the Union soldiers on this line. After their retreat, the Confederates waited for an attack from the Union Army that never came. The Union leadership determined that, as the Yankee forces had also absorbed a high casualty rate from this Confederate assault, the order to charge the Confederate lines that were now in shock from the failed assault never came. The following day, July 4th, 1863, the Rebel forces began their march to their southern territories to regroup and plan other attacks on their northern enemies.

As this man walks in the area where the Confederate forces once assembled to begin their assault on the Union lines, he looks behind him at the beautiful farmland that graces the outskirts of the battlefield. As Confederate Avenue lies very close in proximity to his present position, the man views a tour bus and several cars moving away from the area. As these modern day vehicles pass behind him, he again focuses his attention toward the open field that became the final resting-place for many Rebel forces.

However, as he views the scene before him, he notices a very bizarre sight to the left of the main part of the field. In the sky, toward a small area of trees, he sees many round flashes of light that glow and depart from his view. Closing his eyes and reopening, he again sees several flashes that are obviously brighter than the present day illumination of the battlefield before him. Then, as quickly as this bewildered man viewed this very strange anomaly, the display of lights faded away into nothingness!

Now standing at the site of death totally bewildered, this man thinks about what had just played out before his unbelieving eyes. A quick glance in the direction of the few tourists in the same general area that he occupies tells him that no one else had been the recipient of these strange, ghostly lights.

Ruling out all other possibilities, the man that had experienced the strange happening came to the conclusion that what he had just witnessed was a small part of the massive shelling from the ancient Confederate artillery long since departed for the world of the dead. Artillery that has been silent for many decades. Why, on occasion, does this battle, long since ended, begin again in view of only a select few? The soldiers of the past quite possibly could divulge this information to us all. However, these same soldiers are beyond the reach of the living that take in the sights and sounds of the modern day battlefield at Gettysburg. We only can be assured that the ghostly visions of the past again invade this present day and time as the spirits from beyond the veil of death make their presence known on what is purportedly one of the most haunted battlefields in the United States.

*Exact area on the Gettysburg Battlefield
where strange lights were seen
in the sky.*

Visitation
(Morrisdale, Pennsylvania)

Marcia Hibbard wakes from a restful night's sleep. Looking at the clock that hangs on her mother's living room wall, she is surprised that the time is only 2:30 AM. Wondering what had abruptly caused her to become awake, she reasons that, since she is not in her own bed but is sleeping on the living room couch in her mother's house, the new surroundings might have had something to do with her sudden restlessness.

Then, as quickly as this thought exits her mind, a sound is heard from the near-by kitchen. This, however, is not a sound that she has experienced in her lifetime. When asked what this sound resembled, she stated that the closest thing that she could think of was the sound that one hears when someone runs his or her hand down a closed window blind.

As this sound was remarkably loud, Marcia's mother, who was sleeping in a nearby room, yells to her daughter to "keep the racket down!" Marcia, however, yells back to her mother that she wasn't the one causing the strange, loud sounds.

Nothing more is heard by Marcia or her mother this night. However, when Marcia wakes the next morning, she

55

decides to investigate what the strange sound might have been. In a very short time her mother, too, begins her search of what the strange sound might have been.

After considerable investigation, the two bewildered people decide that, what they had heard in the dead of the night was the sound of someone, or something, flipping papers that are located in a large box in the kitchen. The sound that was made when Marcia picked up a stack of papers in the box and quickly let them shuffle through her hands was indeed the sound that was heard the night before.

Now, with a certain amount of fear beginning to grip each of them, Marcia and her mother immediately knew who had ruffled the papers in the middle of the night. Since no one was in the kitchen when the incident happened, it didn't take each person much thought to come to the conclusion that the sound was made by Marcia's Great Uncle Joe. Since the papers were his, along with the fact that some of the materials in the papers were of sentimental value, it was concluded that Joe was again visiting the kitchen that held his belongings.

The only problem with this solution to the sounds in the night was that Joe had been dead for quite some time! No other explanation could be found to account for the strange sounds in the night. Joe had apparently come back one last time to look over some of his belongings that he wouldn't need in the world beyond this one.

Interstate 99 Ghost

(Altoona, Pennsylvania)

Completed in 1995, the stretch of road that connects the city of Altoona with Tyrone, Pennsylvania, has seen numerous accidents over its short life-span. The following story could, quite possibly, be documentation of an entity that refuses to leave its area of demise.

On the date of July 6, 2003, it was a gorgeous summer day. I lived in the Grassflat, Pennsylvania area (45 minutes west of State College, PA) and decided to take a shopping trip to Altoona to purchase Russian Sage plants for my flower garden.

As I was returning home on the Bud Shuster I99 highway, I had only gone a short distance, perhaps one and one half to two miles, when suddenly my attention was drawn to the front passenger side window of my car. The window was tightly closed. However, between the front side of the window and the door frame near the windshield, a gray, cloud-like form was sliding like a thin sheet of paper into my car!

As it entered, it floated into the passenger seat, taking on the form of a person in the form of a shapely cloud. It filled the entire passenger-side front seat and sat there

57

comfortably, much like a human being. The entity took on the form of a human with a head, body, arms, and legs totally visible to me. As it sat next to me in the passenger side area of my car, it never attempted to make eye contact with me. Therefore, I did not see the front view of this entity that decided to ride with me on my trip home. I merely viewed the side of its features. During this time of visitation, my automobile was engaged in the cruise-control mode, therefore, I was free to gaze upon this being from another world for quite some time.

While I sat gazing at this most bizarre sight, I immediately thought of a sister that had passed away several years earlier. As these thoughts entered my mind, I assumed that the ghostly apparition that was now a passenger in my car was indeed my long lost sister that had passed on to the world beyond.

With this thought deeply etched in my mind, I experienced no fear. On the contrary, I was exuberant that this person from the dead that now entered my life might indeed be my loving sister that I had missed for so long. With this surprising feeling of jubilation, I looked over at the entity that was now sharing my ride home and exclaimed, "Oh, so you're riding with me today Margaret?" However, as I immediately finished my attempted conversation with what I thought was my long dead sister, the entity immediately rose like a cloud and floated to the rear seat of my car!

Now, in full realization that what had been occupying my passenger side seat was probably not my sister, as the being was much too large to have been my long lost sister, I immediately sensed an intense fear beginning to grip my very soul. However, I forced myself to keep my eyes on the highway before me as I didn't want to view this strange person that was now somewhere in the backseat of my car. I would not glance in my rear-view mirror nor turn my head to view behind me as I didn't think that I could bear the sight that I might see if I turned to view my ghostly passenger. I didn't want to know if the passenger from beyond the grave might have exited my car via my rear window or if it was still occupying the rear portion of my now speeding vehicle.

Upon arriving home, I exited my vehicle and, after gaining enough nerve, viewed the back seat of my car to see if the entity might still be located there. However, as I looked throughout my car, I didn't see anything ghostly that I thought I might see. The back seat of my car that, at one time, was occupied by an entity that I didn't recognize, was thankfully empty!

I shall never forget my frightful trip from Altoona with the ghostly apparition that decided to travel the long, lonesome trail with me on Interstate 99!

(The previous story was mainly written word for word as it was received by the author. Very minor changes were made within the story.)

There have been numerous deaths in the area associated with travel on Interstate 99. Could one of the people that so tragically lost their life on I99 have been the passenger in the car that traveled from the Altoona area to worlds beyond?

Haunted Interstate 99?

The Light
(Morrisdale, Pennsylvania and Penns Creek, Central PA)

Much has been written about the phenomenon known as the near-death experience, or simply NDE as it is sometimes known. This is a happening in which a clinically dead person immediately views an intensely bright light on a pathway to what is described as intense love and happiness. Then, with the modern techniques of today to bring a human back from death via the medical profession, the deceased is now placed back among the living. However, many times this now revived person begins to tell of their exhilarating experience while they were beckoned toward the light.

Is the light that is observed by many that have experienced this phenomenon the gateway to Heaven? Is this our Creator waiting to welcome us into our Heavenly Reward?

On various occasions, strange lights are also seen by the living in the form of ghostly encounters. Are these illuminations also from Heaven and ultimately from God? Consider the story that was given to me by a person that resides in the small central Pennsylvania town of Morrisdale. In this strange account, a young girl, about the age of 19, was saddened by the fact that her grandfather was about to pass away at a local hospital. After she had said her prayers for her grandfather, she fell asleep into what was to become a night that she would never forget. As she slept, a beautiful, bright light began to illuminate her bedroom! As she woke in the middle of the night, the intense light bathed her in a beautiful glow that startled the girl. However, as this intense burst of light seemed to have no source for the illumination that it gave, the young girl became frightened, closed her eyes and quickly pulled her covers over her head. As she did so, the beautiful light immediately ceased.

Some time after this episode, the girl felt safe enough to leave her room and scurry to her mother's room. As she entered her mother's room, the girl told of the strange light that had entered her part of the house as she slept. Also, the young girl had a very strong feeling that her grandfather had just passed away.

In what was a very strange outcome, the family did receive a phone call from the hospital where the girl's grandfather was being cared for. The doctor that relayed the news of the grandfather's death gave the exact time of death as the time when the strange light entered the girl's room in the middle of the night!

Was this light that seemingly came from no-where the girl's grandfather visiting his granddaughter one last time before he left this earth for the world to come? Or, was this strange light an angel of God, sent not only to bring news of the man's death but also a sign that the girl's grandfather had indeed crossed over to his Heavenly Reward?

Ghosts! of Pennsylvania

Other, more ominous lights have been reported by individuals when a loved one is nearing the journey to the world of the dead. An older gentleman from central Pennsylvania offered a story that has traveled through the years within his family about a strange being of light that was witnessed by two members of his family. In a small home near Penns Creek, Centre County, a young brother and sister walked the small dirt road that led to their grandfather's home. The path that led to the small home was very dark as it was now the dead of night and they carried no lantern to illuminate the way. As they walked through the wooded area that led to the home, they saw something up ahead of them. A bright glow that formed into the likeness of a human being carrying a lantern walked ahead of them at a brisk pace! Startled by this ghostly figure, the couple stopped in their tracks and watched as the brightly-lit figure floated to their grand-dad's home. Still observing this frightening sight, the two thoroughly scared people watched as the specter floated onto the porch of the grandfather's home and immediately disappeared.

As the couple approached the home, they saw not a trace of the strange being of light. Also, as they entered the home to visit their ill grandfather, they did not observe the ghostly being anywhere in their sight. After visiting their grandfather for quite some time, they left to walk the long road to their parent's home. This time, however, the two bewildered individuals walked a bit faster through the dense, dark forest that surrounded their road to safely.

The following day, with thoughts of the strange, ghostly being still etched in their minds, it was divulged to them that their grandfather had died sometime that night. They had known that their grandfather had become very ill but they were unaware that his illness would lead to his death.

Some time after his death, the two youths related their story of the strange being of light that they had experienced only hours before their grandfather's death. Some believed that this ghostly being might have actually been an angel, sent by God, to assist their ill grandfather to Heaven. Others claimed that, as the specter was in human form and carried a lantern, that this ghostly being might have been one of their long-dead relatives coming to take their grandfather home.

Whatever this strange being from another dimension was, the family of the deceased grandfather will never forget the tale of the ghostly being for as long as they live. When asked about his view of the specter bathed in light, the person that related this story to me simply stated, "We think of the Light of Life (God). This was sort of the light of death!"

The Ultimate Visitation
(Rural Centre County, Pennsylvania)

An obviously elated, albeit bewildered, man of God looks out over his congregation in rural Centre County, Pennsylvania. What this preacher has just been witness to has not stirred the hearers of his sermon. The apparition that he has just had the pleasure of viewing was meant for him and him alone. He immediately wonders, was his prayer answered?

There comes a time in every person's life when thoughts of the afterlife enter our thoughts. Are we pleasing our Creator in this life or should we attempt to change certain aspects of our daily living? Will I reach Heaven or am I destined for a much more sinister place, a place of extreme torment?

Reverend Daniel Howe began to think of his calling to his present Godly profession many years in the past. After years of witnessing to the truth, he began to wonder about his devotion to his calling. Was this his true calling in this life and, if so, did his Creator think highly of his service to Him?

After much contemplation, Daniel decided to pray and ask his Maker to divulge to him if the Powers above were pleased with his witnessing throughout the many years that he had devoted to his profession. Feeling that he was in need of a "spiritual lift," he prayed that a sign from Heaven might be given to him that would confirm the Almighty's positive feelings toward his devoted servant.

Life continued on as usual after Reverend Daniel's heartfelt prayer. Every week he readied his sermon to be given at various churches throughout Clearfield and Centre counties. However, on a very special day in a small country church in rural Centre county, Reverend Howe received a very strong and loving answer to the prayer that he had prayed in days past.

As Reverend Howe stood outside the small country church in which he was to preach this Sunday morning, he immediately noticed the beauty of the building as well as the surroundings that invited all believers to enter this humble, yet beautiful House of God. The church was situated on a small knoll and was shaded by an obviously very old, large oak tree. As he entered the church to prepare for Sunday services, Reverend Daniel stared at the empty pews inside this country church and wondered if his ministry was as beneficial to his congregation as he hoped it was.

As he sat in the front part of the church and contemplated how he would very shortly deliver his message of God, he couldn't help but notice the many people that now began to fill the small structure. Pleased with the amount of followers that he would minister to on this day, he walked the short distance to the altar of the church and began to preach.

After many minutes of witnessing to the congregation, his attention was immediately diverted to the right side of the church. Hardly believing what his eyes and mind were

telling him, he observed a very bright light that hovered halfway down the extreme right isle of the church! The intensely bright light only lasted but a second. However, as his mind began to replay the prayer that he had uttered some time ago, he immediately knew that God had indeed answered his heartfelt prayer in the form of the apparition that he just had the pleasure to observe. Was this an angel sent to confirm that God was pleased with his servant's mission? Or, was this truly the Son of God himself, appearing very briefly to this humble man of God, to instill a new vigor within him?

Standing at the pulpit with a sense of bewilderment engulfing him, Reverend Daniel Howe observed his congregation. There was not a person in the church that had experienced the blinding light, none except him as all eyes were still fixed on this elated preacher!

After the services were completed, Reverend Howe thanked God for the loving answer to his prayer that he had completed many days before the visitation from Heaven.

Reverend Howe was indeed pleasing God with his witnessing to the many parishioners that heard him preach.

When asked if his answered prayer had changed his life, Reverend Howe exclaimed, "I felt like I was walking on cloud-nine for awhile!" No recipient of a mere ghostly apparition can claim such exhilaration.

Church Of Lights
(Gettysburg, Pennsylvania)

The Gettysburg landscape, as it is viewed today, is much different than it was when the famous battle commenced in July of 1863. Many of the buildings and trees that the soldiers viewed in the mid-1800s are now also a part of history.

However, there are several Civil War era structures that still remain for all visitors of this battlefield to enjoy. Many of the structures that still remain from 1863 were undoubtedly pressed into service as either shelters for soldiers fighting the battle or the much needed Civil War hospitals that saw so much pain and anguish in those days of war. Included in this list of buildings still standing from the great battle are at least two places of worship. As these houses of the holy were used as Civil War hospitals during the Battle of Gettysburg, each church obviously holds immense amounts of history within its walls. When visiting the town of Gettysburg, these structures should also be viewed, in addition to walking the actual battlefield, as there is also a great deal of historical significance associated with these buildings.

In at least one of these Civil War era churches, a man from central Pennsylvania discovered that the structure itself held more than mere history. He found, as he attended services on a bright summer morning, that the ghosts of the Gettysburg dead also inhabit these structures! As the man entered his place of worship away from his hometown, he couldn't help but think of the many soldiers that entered this structure during the Battle of Gettysburg and exited as only a shell of a body without a soul.

Finding a seat close to the rear of the church, he began to notice that the church was unusually full for a Sunday morning service. All other times in which he had attended services at this church, before proceeding to the battlefield, he always had his choice of seating. On this day, however, there was an abundance of worshipers present in addition to himself.

As the Sunday morning services began, he noticed nothing out of the ordinary. The congregation sang the opening hymn as he continued on with his thoughts of this Civil War era building.

Half way through the service, however, a very strange episode began to unfold before his very eyes. As he viewed the front altar of the church he noticed, only a short distance to the left of the altar, two very small lights zigzagging on one of the side beams that supported the church! As he viewed this un-ordinary sight, he immediately thought that someone must have opened the rear doors of the church to cause these bizarre lights to dart about so wildly. However, when he turned to view the doors behind him, not a person was in the back of the church to do anything, let alone open the doors.

Now quickly turning toward the front of the church, he failed to see the strange wisps of light that he had previously encountered only moments before. Shaking his head in disbelief, the man again began to worship with the congregation.

However, after a very brief time, he again saw the strange lights emanating from...beyond! This time, however, the fast-moving lights had moved to near the ceiling of the church. Now in full realization that these strange, darting lights were not of this world, the man became entranced by their movements. After some time of viewing this ghostly illumination, the lights immediately and without warning blinked out for the final time!

When asked what he perceived these strange lights to have been, the man stated that he felt that he had viewed a small piece of the paranormal that so many talk about at Gettysburg. Also, he stated that, since he was inside a structure that was used as a Civil War hospital during the actual battle, the only explanation that he could think of for the eerie lights was that they were the dead that had expired in this building during the Battle of Gettysburg. Whatever these strange lights were, after ruling out all possibilities, there doesn't seem to be an explanation that seems to fit, other than the explanation of the Civil War dead that again made their presence known in an old Civil War era building.

*A view of the town of Gettysburg from atop
the tower on Culp's Hill. Is this truly a highly charged
paranormal town that many speak of?*

Native Soil
(Gettysburg, Pennsylvania)

Long before the battle of Gettysburg and long before the white man settled in the area, the parcel of land that holds so many memories and feelings was inhabited by Native Americans. Little did these native people realize that their home would one day become a field of death the likes had never been seen before.

Not realizing that the area in and around Devil's Den and the Triangular Field was once inhabited by Native Americans, Betsy Komo and her mother Ann ventured into the unknown of the Gettysburg Battlefield. Their trek took the two visitors of the hallowed grounds to the area around Devil's Den as mother and daughter continually spoke of the great battle that caused so much death and destruction many decades in the past. As Ann exclaimed that she was feeling a bit weary, she decided to sit on one of the many large boulders that cover the ground behind Devil's Den and stretch her tired legs. Betsy, not willing to give up so easy on such a beautiful fall day, decided to leave her mother and explore the near-by confines of the Triangular Field.

73

Ghosts! of Pennsylvania

As Ann relaxed on the large rock, she watched as her daughter descended lower and lower into the Triangular Field. Suddenly and without warning Ann's ears became filled with a very strange sound that made her feel a bit uneasy. As she watched her daughter disappear into the field below, the ghostly sound of what could only be described as an Indian tribal dance filled her ears. Ghostly chanting and the beating of a distant drum in unison with the weird chanting became almost unbearable to Ann.

Now deciding to cover her ears to hopefully escape the strange sounds, the ghostly sounds made by something other than the Union and Confederate soldiers from times past suddenly ceased. As Ann opened her eyes and uncovered her ears, she found her daughter standing in front of her with a quizzical look etched across her face. Betsy had witnessed her mother acting in a peculiar manner and wondered what had happened to her after she had left to explore the Triangular Field.

After telling her tale of what could only be described as ghostly chants and drumbeats, Ann's daughter chuckled to her mother and stated "You have the wrong conflict mom! This is the Battle of Gettysburg, not Custer's Last Stand!" However, Betsy's mother had the last laugh in this exchange between mother and daughter as it was found that long before the Great Battle, the area that the two tread upon was inhabited by Native Americans.

Various people that delve into the paranormal on the battlefield at Gettysburg have reported ghostly drums piercing the air at Devil's Den. Upon hearing these strange sounds emanating from another time, some tourists to this great battlefield go back to the year 1863 and hear the drums and cries of battle that once echoed through the jumble of boulders around the area. However, on occasion, some bewildered visitors to the Battlefield at Gettysburg reach back a bit further in time and experience the ghosts of a people long departed from this truly historic area.

Area behind Devil's Den where ghostly chants were heard.

Peaceful Glow
(Philipsburg, Pennsylvania)

A young man sleeps peacefully in a home that he had acquired through inheritance. A small smile graces his lips as he falls deeply into a restful sleep. You see, this man has just touched a small piece of the paranormal through a ghostly encounter. As most hauntings and experiences with ghosts are typically frightening, this case of an otherworldly encounter holds a much deeper meaning than most encounters with spirits of the dead. The man that has just experienced ghostly activity in his home feels very fortunate to have had such an encounter. Many encounters with his resident ghost have happened to him through the year that he has owned the home. This ghost, however, is a bit different in his mind. He not only feels that his specter is friendly, but he also feels that this spirit of a long dead soul offers protection to him in the form of ghostly assurance.

The man's most recent encounter plays out much like other encounters that he receives. As he climbs the darkened stairway to his bedroom he notices nothing out of the ordinary. However, some time after he extinguishes his night light, the spirit of a former owner of the house makes his presence known. Although the man has never actually seen his ghostly friend, he nevertheless knows that he is with him.

On this warm, summer night the man lays on his bed with his eyes closed when his most recent experience begins. First, footsteps can be heard on the staircase just outside his locked bedroom door. He knows that he should not show any fear, as these sounds are not made by any earthly intruder. Some time later, as the man waits silently in the dark room, he experiences yet another ghostly happening. With eyes closed he senses a very bright flash of light that causes him to quickly open his eyes. However, as in past nights, he views nothing. The extremely bright flash dissipates as quickly as it had come.

Then, as he calms himself again to attempt to sleep, he experiences the most gentle of final hauntings for this night. As he lies very still, he feels the gentle pull of an unknown hand at his blanket. This will be the final presence that the man experiences on this night, the same as in nights past.

Most experiences with the paranormal normally cause great fear to the recipient of the haunting. However, on occasion, a very benevolent and protective apparition can be experienced by an unsuspecting soul. Are these seemingly helpful apparitions truly ghosts attempting to secure the friendship of an earthly inhabitant or are they something a bit more? A Guardian Angel perhaps? One can only wonder at the true meaning of the otherworldly forces at work in some of our earthly homes.

House Of Many Haunts
(Clarion County, Pennsylvania)

It seems that an earth bound ghost has the option to use whatever senses it deems appropriate when making contact with the living. The most common type of haunting seems to be auditory in nature when hearing reports of ghostly activity. An unsuspecting person hears something in another room or other area that is vacant only to find, upon entering the area, nothing to be found. Usually, in cases like this, the ghostly sounds subside before the person enters the area of the haunting. However, this is only one form of haunting that many individuals experience. Visits from the dead also come in the form of ghostly contact in the form of a touch or shove or push. Also, the olfactory nerves of smell are not to be left out as this author has also experienced this form of haunting. Last, but certainly not the least bizarre form of haunting, is the actual sighting of a deceased person. This form of haunting usually enters a person's mind and soul in an all too realistic and striking way.

However, not to be left out are the many photographs and audio recordings of specters that grace the pages of books and various web-sites. While many of these photos and recordings submitted for all to view and hear can be explained as normal phenomena, some truly can't be disproved as ghostly apparitions.

A family that resides near the town of Knox, Pennsylvania has witnessed many of the aforementioned styles of hauntings within their home. Lori Salem, her husband Will and their children have all been recipients of the many spirits that they claim inhabit their home.

Built in the early 1920's, the Salem's home has seen its share of tragedy. In the late 1930's, the original owner of the home was murdered within the confines of the structure before departing for a Christmas party. Before leaving for the party, the owner of the home was in the barn feeding his animals before tragedy struck. While in the barn, the man's neighbor entered the home and shot the man's 14-year-old son in the kitchen. Seeing this unbelievable scene unfolding before her eyes, the man's young daughter ran out of the house and into the barn to inform her father to what had just happened. Upon entering the house, the father was almost immediately killed by the crazed neighbor in the dining room of the home. After this murder, the young girl ran out of the house and into the family's car for protection from the gunman. The man's wife and other daughter, after viewing the bloody scene, ran upstairs and attempted to barricade themselves in an upper room.

The gun-wielding neighbor then attempted to kill the daughter that had escaped into the car. After shooting through the side window of the auto, the young girl slumped over, apparently dead. However, this brave soul had the presence of mind to fake her death, even while being wounded by the man's shot.

Meanwhile, the mother and her other daughter managed to open an upstairs window, climb onto a porch roof, jump off of the porch to the ground below and run into the safety of the nearby woods.

Shortly after these gruesome murders, the man that carried out the evil deeds was apprehended in Seneca, Pennsylvania. After this horrible day of death, the home sat vacant for a number of years. The home eventually was inhabited again and, over the years, had only a small number of families move into and out of the residence. Then, Lori Salem, her husband Will and their family bought the house and attempted to settle into what proved to be a very haunted residence!

As families move into new places to call their own, an initial adjustment period usually follows that sometimes takes months, if not years for some families. However, in Lori and Will's case, this period of adjustment to their new home and the ghostly presence that co-inhabits their residence continues to this very day.

In speaking with Lori, she stated that her family has had so many haunting experiences that she didn't know which happenings to outline first. She did, however, state that the month of August seems to bring with it a sharp increase in paranormal activity. To her, this seems strange as the murders that had taken place so many years in the past happened on December 27. Could all of the hauntings of their home be the work of the poor souls that so tragically lost their lives on that post Christmas day so many decades ago? Or, are those souls intermingled with others that have owned the property throughout the years?

One of the strange happenings that played out in recent times includes the probable visitation of a young friend that only seems to want to play with the Salem's young children.

One day a young neighbor boy came to visit Lori and Will's small child. The Salem's child played downstairs while the neighbor went upstairs to play. Shortly after the boy entered the upstairs area, he was seen running down the staircase that led to the rooms downstairs. He called to Lori's son that there was a little boy upstairs and that he wanted to play. Lori's son immediately called to his mother to ask if it was OK to go upstairs with the neighbor and play with what Lori thought might have been an imaginary friend. Lori told the two boys to go upstairs and play but to come down immediately when she called them, as their lunch was almost ready.

After approximately 15 minutes, Lori called the two boys and they promptly entered the kitchen to eat their meal. When Lori asked what had happened to their little playmate, the boys exclaimed that he also had to go home. He was never seen again or heard about again. Before one reasons this potential haunting to a child's need for the fantasy of a childhood "imaginary friend," when asked about this possibility, Lori stated that she didn't think that her son and their neighbor were "making up" the story as the two boys never talked about their little friend again. Also, during the first two weeks of their inhabitation of the home, the family heard many times in the still of the night, the sound of a little boy's feet running up and down the upstairs hallway. However, when one would attempt to investigate, not a soul from this side of Heaven or the next could be found!

Someone or something running in the upstairs hallway at night continued to be a common occurrence in the Salem's home until one late night, after attempting to sleep, Lori entered the hallway, saw nothing but yelled to the invisible intruder, "I've had it! It's dark; it's nighttime! If you want to run in the hallway, do it during the day when I'm not here!" After this desperate confrontation with what the family believes is the ghost of a little boy, only occasional unexplained walking is heard by the family at night. Could this restless spirit of a little boy assume that Mrs. Salem is his long dead mother and listen to her pleas for silence?

The ghost of a young boy is not the only earthbound soul that occasionally makes his presence known to the Salem family. An older man has also made his presence known in the form of a very lifelike apparition!

Lori's four-year-old son was playing in the living room while she was again preparing food in the kitchen. Suddenly, the son burst into the kitchen and yelled to his mother that there was a strange man in the house. The young boy told his bewildered mother that a man had just come down the stairs and had gone THROUGH the front door! After Lori and her husband searched the entire home as well as the entire outside boundaries of their home, they found not a clue to what could have invaded their home. However, when asked what the man looked like and what type and style of clothes the man wore, the original home-owner's daughter stated that the man the young boy claimed to have seen resembles her father exactly! Once again, could this have been the vivid imagination of a little boy? There seem to be too many coincidences to disprove his story.

Another encounter with the strange specter of a man happened to Lori in the early morning hours of an August day. While still in bed, Lori heard the distinct sounds of a man talking downstairs. Immediately thinking that the voice must be coming from her husband readying himself for work, she looked at the clock that sat on her night-stand beside her bed. After seeing that the time was now 7AM, Lori immediately thought that her husband should have left for work long before this time so she decided to investigate the source of the strange voice. After rising from her bed, Lori proceeded down the home's staircase and was taken aback to see a man dressed in what appeared to be a baker's uniform sitting on their chair! As their eyes met, the man casually got up and walked out of the room through the kitchen door! Shaking her head in disbelief at what she had just witnessed, Lori ran to the kitchen and found nothing! The ghostly apparition had again made his presence known and had simply vanished without a trace!

When asked how many souls the family might have "living" with them, Lori stated that the family has seen three life-like apparitions but they believe that possibly five ghostly figures inhabit their home.

As stated at the beginning of this story that there are various types of haunting presences that one can observe, Lori closed with two other unexplainable tales that involved the sense of smell. In her bedroom, she became overcome with sickness one morning after smelling the distinct odor of a hair-spray that she finds awful! Needless to say, no one in the home uses this brand of hair-spray that has been on the market for years. Did one of the spirits use this brand of hair-spray when they were alive? Lori stated that she would not have this brand of spray in her home so, what other possibility would there be to explain the ghostly smell. Also, Lori reported that recently the strong smell of cigarette smoke has been filling their home even though no one in their family smokes!

As with various other encounters that have been reported, Lori and her family feel no threat from the apparitions that make their presence known in their haunted residence. They, too, feel that the spirits of the long departed dead mean no harm to their family. In fact, the family feels a protective presence with the new ghostly additions to their family!

Forms Of Terror
(Gettysburg, Pennsylvania)

Many tourists from varying parts of the country congregated at and near the Triangular Field on the Battlefield at Gettysburg. Tim Hudson was one of the many visitors to the battlefield that were not only immersed in the dense historic quality of the place but also found time to take the occasional photo of his favorite Civil War park.

As Tim walked the terrain of the Triangular Field, he couldn't help but reminisce about the many men that died terrible deaths within view of his present position. As Tim sat quietly on the stone wall that marks the area where Union soldiers fired upon Confederate forces at the top of the Triangular Field, an old man entered his area of view and proceeded toward Tim near the stone wall. As the old gent neared, he waved at Tim and gave a verbal greeting to the younger man. As Tim was a very cordial young man, he welcomed conversation with any who might want to speak to him about the Battle of Gettysburg or anything else that others might want to talk about.

Tim hoped, however, that this kindly man would offer some insight into the great battle that he hadn't heard or read before. Luckily for Tim, this was the case as the man offered some information about the battle that Tim had never heard or read. However, the unique insight that the man offered was totally unexpected. Tim had thought that the man that had approached him only moments before would speak of the many Confederate men that secured the top of the Triangular Field and Devil's Den; or of the many Union forces and guns that had attempted to repel the attack on their position by the Southerners. However, what Tim heard from the older man was unexpected, to say the least. The man immediately asked Tim if he had ever heard the stories of the Civil War dead making their presence known on the battlefield and, specifically, on the field that they were now on. Slightly surprised at the old man's question, Tim regained his composure after what he felt was an odd question and responded with his usual grace.

Not only had Tim ever experienced anything out of the ordinary at the Gettysburg Battlefield but he had also never heard anyone speak of any type of paranormal event on the battlefield. After offering to the man that he had never heard of or saw a ghostly apparition on the battlefield, he asked the older man if he had any unexplainable experiences while out on the great field of battle. After stating that he had had his share of moments on the battlefield that he couldn't explain, Tim became glued to every word that this kindly man spoke.

As this man had obviously visited the Battlefield at Gettysburg many times, and in many years gone by in his life, Tim listened attentively to the man's wealth of knowledge with an open mind, although the knowledge that the man offered was something totally new and unexpected to Tim. The man told Tim of many times in the past in which he had seen apparitions of dead Civil War soldiers floating across several areas of the battlefield, undoubtedly preparing for a ghostly battle that never seems to end. He outlined areas on the battlefield where he had seen apparitions, including the Wheatfield, Little Round Top and Devil's Den, and explained to the young man how, after a short period of time, the ghostly forms would disappear into nothingness!

Now thoroughly glued to every word that the man spoke, Tim asked if he had had any strange encounters with the Union and Confederate dead on the field in which they sat. With a small smile, the man offered that he had seen apparitions, strange, ghostly smells and unearthly noises in many areas on the battlefield, including the Triangular Field.

After a bit more conversation with Tim, the old man excused himself, exclaimed how nice it was to have had a conversation with Tim and departed.

Tim, now completely mesmerized and invigorated from the conversation, peered into the field below and wondered if the old man might simply be offering legends that couldn't possibly be true.

After sitting near the Triangular Field for a while longer, Tim decided that it was time to travel to the town of Gettysburg and have a much-needed dinner. After his meal, he decided that he would once again visit the battlefield before the park's closing time of 10 PM.

Ghosts! of Pennsylvania

After visiting several areas of fascination on the battlefield, Tim found that he couldn't erase the words that the old gent had left him with only hours before. Were there really ghosts at the Gettysburg Battlefield and, if so, would he see any or hear any on this moonlit night? As Tim drove his vehicle in front of Devil's Den he noticed that the area appeared devoid of any individuals. This was not surprising to him as this was a Sunday evening and many of the tourists that walked the battlefield by day had undoubtedly gone home by this evening hour.

While Tim steered his vehicle around the very sharp turns that exist behind Devil's Den he couldn't help but think about the old man and his stories of the spiritual warriors that he claimed to have seen. Parking his car between Devil's Den and the Triangular Field, Tim exited his car and slowly walked to the wall at the top of the Triangular Field. During past visits to this area, as well as all other areas of the battlefield, Tim only thought of the great battle that had played out many decades before. The thought of anything out of the paranormal realm never entered his mind.

Tim sat very quietly on the wall at the Triangular Field and tried to imagine what it would be like to experience something out of the ordinary on the battlefield. However, just the thought of seeing a ghostly apparition immediately sent a chill down Tim's spine. He decided that, instead of dwelling on what his fellow tourist had told him concerning ghosts on the battlefield, he would do as he had done many times in the past, take in the sights of the terrain and concentrate on the battle itself.

As Tim rose to exit the Triangular Field he looked at the moon shining brightly overhead and thought what a beautiful night he had chosen to stay on the battlefield a bit longer than usual. However, as he began to walk away from the field of death he heard a most unusual and blood-curdling sound. The distinct echo of a Confederate "rebel-yell" filled his ears! The strange sound had come from the bottom of the Triangular Field and had reached his ears in an instant.

After shaking off the initial fear associated with observing the paranormal, Tim began to reason that someone in the woods below the field was attempting to frighten him with the strange sound.

After a bit of thought, Tim decided that he would confront the prankster and uncover the origin of the bizarre sound. Tim again retraced his footsteps into the Triangular Field and beyond as he quietly walked the short distance to the bottom of the field. However, Tim thought, what if the old man was right and there truly were ghostly apparitions visible on the battlefield from time to time? As this thought entered his mind, he decided to stop and re-climb the strange terrain of the field and drive to another place on the battlefield. However, as he turned, Tim heard a sound in the brush below the field. Immediately turning, he began to view a strange fog-like haze that rose and moved horizontally along the lower part of the field.

With eyes now glued to the fog, Tim's senses immediately elevated as the fog began to take on a very loose shape of a man! Now thinking that this scene was just a bit too much for him, Tim turned from the specter and ran as fast as his legs would carry him up the small incline of the haunted field. However, as he turned while he reached the top of the field, he could have sworn that he now saw several fog-like beings moving at slow speeds and at varying angles at the field below!

As Tim reached his car, he didn't possess the bravery to look down into the field again. Thankfully for him, even if he did gain an amount of courage, he could not have viewed the bottom of the Triangular Field, as the incline of the field itself is too steep to have been viewed from that angle.

As Tim sped away in his vehicle, he thought of stopping at the Wheatfield to see if there was anything out of the ordinary taking place at that sight. However, as he passed the Wheatfield (one of the main areas of the second day's fighting at Gettysburg) he decided that the only area he wanted to see was the area inside of his home with his door securely locked behind him!

*View from the bottom of the
Triangular Field*

Icy Touch Of Death
(Bellefonte, Pennsylvania)

Oftentimes, our domestic animals can sense the presence of people, potentially dangerous situations or the otherworldly forms of ghostly apparitions even when our human minds can't. Cats seem to be the most receptive to the unknown. Bob Lyle and his wife Jill can attest to the fact that their friendly feline Mittens oftentimes seems to view things in their home that seemingly only she can see.

One evening while watching television, Bob and Jill became slightly alarmed when their cat began exhibiting very peculiar behavior. Mittens, who was quietly taking a nap on the back of the couch where her owners sat, suddenly rose very quickly from her deep sleep, leapt from the couch and began staring very nervously at the front doorway of the Lyle's home. Seemingly every hair on her back was standing on end as she stared at the doorway! Then, while they were still looking at the door that Mittens obviously had a deep interest in, the eerie sounds of a person walking filled the ears of the two bewildered people! Then, as quickly as the footsteps began, they ceased, at the edge of the doorway. As Bob and Jill looked at each-other in disbelief at the surprising behavior that their cat

92

was exhibiting followed by the strange footsteps, Bob
motioned to his wife that he was going to quietly open the
door into where they had heard the footsteps only moments
before. As Bob and Jill were the only ones in the house at
the time, Bob wondered what he might find on the other
side of the door as he edged closer and closer to his
destination.

As Bob reached for the doorknob before him, he noticed
that their cat's eyes were still glued to the door and
whatever might be on the other side. However, as Bob

quickly opened the
door, he stared at
nothing! Not a soul
occupied the space
where the couple had
heard footsteps only
moments before.

As he shut the
door, Bob stated to his
wife Jill that their
children must not have
been dreaming. You
see, their children

often complained that they had also heard strange, ghostly
footsteps in their home but, upon investigating the area
where the footsteps were heard, could find nothing!

Several years later, the Lyles planned a vacation that
would take them away from the area for a few days. After
securing the services of a person that worked for them to
look in on their home and to feed their cat while they were

away, the whole family ventured far away from their Bellefonte home to enjoy their time away.

All went well for the young man that was caring for the home for the first two days. However, on the third day of caring for the Lyles' home and cat, this young helper would experience something in the home that he would not soon forget.

As he was finished with the duties of feeding and watering the Lyles' cat, the man began his short walk to the front door to exit the home. However, as he turned the doorknob to open the door, he encountered a happening with the paranormal that made him run from the haunted residence. As he attempted to open the door, the young man felt the icy touch of a very cold hand on his shoulder. However, as he turned to see who or what was causing this eerie sensation, he was surprised to see nothing but an empty room behind him!

As this cold touch of presumably a ghostly apparition filled his senses, he immediately ran from the home after hurriedly locking the front door behind him.

After the Lyles returned home, the young man informed his employers that he would never step into their home again! When asked why, the excited man told of the icy touch of something not of this world that caused him to run from the residence.

As Bob and Jill heard the story of the man's encounter with an obvious entity that inhabits their home, they thought back to the many times that their children heard footsteps within their home and also their one evening of fright as their cat warned them of the ghostly intruder. After hearing the strange story from the young man, they both wondered why no one in their family had been the victim of the cold touch of the ghostly person. Were they just lucky that they weren't singled out for physical haunting by the unseen force? Or, was the entity simply protecting their home from what he or she thought was an intruder? In either case, no explanation for the strange happenings in the Lyles' home was ever found.

Stillness Of The Wheatfield

(Gettysburg, Pennsylvania)

The Wheatfield on the battlefield at Gettysburg lies quiet. On this day in late October, 2002, a single family parks their SUV and embarks on an adventure that will live on in their lives for eternity; a lesson in history that one can't receive from a mere book of history.

On the second day of the Battle of Gettysburg, a much different scenario met the multitude of soldiers from the North and South as the crackle of a multitude of weaponry as well as the agonizing cries of the wounded and dying filled the air.

On this day, however, one could hear a pin drop as the extremely quiet Wheatfield beckoned this western Pennsylvania family to visit its borders.

As the family exited their vehicle, their two children began to run toward the many monuments that the Wheatfield has to offer. Mother and father, however, strolled at a much more leisurely pace as their children became further and further from their view.

Upon reaching the area where their children were now, the mother and father noticed that their young children were

96

attempting to climb up and onto one of the memorials to the Gettysburg battle. After re-directing her children concerning the dangers of climbing on the monuments, the children again ran to a still further area on this killing field of the past. However, as the children ran and their parents watched, a most unfamiliar sound pierced the once still air. In the distance, as all members of this family stopped their movements, the

unmistakable sound of a lone horse galloping at full stride filled the ears of this now bewildered family. Are horses allowed in this area of

the battlefield, they wondered? And, if so, they felt that the rider of this large animal should be reported to the Park Service due to the extremely dangerous speed at which the horse and rider were traveling.

As the mother and father realized that the galloping became nearer and nearer to their position on the Wheatfield, both parents immediately began to call their frightened children to run to them and the relative safety that they would attempt to provide. However, as the children reached their parents, the sound of the galloping horse immediately ceased! As everyone looked at each-other in disbelief, they all wondered aloud what had happened to the horse and rider that had, only moments before, apparently reached a position on the Wheatfield in close proximity to where the family now stood.

After many minutes of intense listening, only a very soft breeze could be heard and felt by the mesmerized family of four. After this ghostly episode with the dead at Gettysburg, the family jogged to their waiting SUV and left the area of the Wheatfield in total disbelief at what they had just witnessed. It was decided by all that they would continue their tour of the battlefield this day, but only in the safety of their vehicle. Their shoes would not touch the hallowed ground of the battlefield again on this visit!

Many other strange accounts of ghostly activity have been reported by various individuals at the Wheatfield at Gettysburg, including strange blue mist that attempts to form into living soldiers of the past, strange, ghostly smells of long ago and the actual sounds of battle seemingly brought in on the gentle breezes that engulf this vast field of death. The breeze that met the frightened family of four on this day, however, was a horse and rider of many decades ago that simply dematerialized before the four could glimpse their wild ride into destiny.

*The famous once bloody Wheatfield
on the Battlefield At Gettysburg
as viewed from the Irish
Brigade monument.*

"Ghost Investigations 101"

Before beginning any type of paranormal investigation or "ghost hunt," always remember to ask permission to be on any property that is considered private. Also, when on this property, or any other property, please be respectful of the buildings or terrain that you will be walking on or into to conduct your investigation.

There are no tried and true methods to conduct your own paranormal investigation. However, begin by taking into consideration the area in which you have a desire to conduct your investigation. Some important questions to ask yourself are, is this place purportedly haunted based on other's eyewitness accounts? Has your area of interest been the sight of either a violent or "quick" death or deaths? Is the place that you have an interest in an area of tragedy? If your answer is yes to any of the aforementioned questions, you might be surprised at what you might uncover during your investigation.

Old, abandoned buildings (especially former homes) and cemeteries are very good possibilities for beginning your investigation. Also, as in the case of several stories in this book, battlefields in which premature death became commonplace might be a unique starting point in which to begin your investigation.

There are a number of devices to press into service to begin your "ghost hunt." However, I have found that the simplest of devices work as well as any high-tech "gadgets" that so-called professional ghost hunters use. Two favorite devices that are used by many on the Gettysburg Battlefield are a simple camera (35mm or any digital camera will work nicely) and/ or some type of taping device. When I take photos of purportedly haunted areas, I oftentimes discard any photo that shows the presence of orbs. I have found that there are so many things that could cause an orb to appear on your film, I must question the validity of this type of "ghost." However, you might feel otherwise. This is entirely up to the discretion of each individual.

The other simple device that can be pressed into service is any type of recording device. When using these devices, please be sure that a fresh tape is used during each and every investigation as, when one uses tapes that have already been used, overlap of audio could result.

When you use your recorder on a selected area, simply switch on the tape during a time when little or no noise can be heard in the background. Then, either attempt to speak to whatever might be out there, stay very quiet or walk away and come back when you believe that the tape might be completed.

There have been many recordings of strange voices using this simple method. Some of the voices that are heard resemble garbled and indiscernible audio. However, unless you have some type of background noise that could have made these sounds, you might just have succeeded in your experiment. Oftentimes, these garbled voices begin to make sense if you have the capability to either slow your tape or speed the tape up.

However, many times when attempting to record a ghostly voice on tape, you will be astonished to obtain just that, a ghostly voice on tape!

But, most importantly, be patient. When conducting your investigation you might not receive any voice on your recording device or the presence of anything on your film. This is more common than some would have you believe. Also, please be a bit skeptical when you think that you have captured something either on tape or on film. Please be certain to rule out all possibilities for what you see or hear. Only then can you be quite certain that you might just have copied something from the world of the dead attempting to make his or her presence known!

Lastly, please do not dabble in the occult. Please do not seek the services of "mediums" or psychics, or attempt to use an ouija board to conduct investigations. We are not, as children of God, to use such items.

Mountain Hauntings
(Altoona, Pennsylvania)

The many hills and mountains in central Pennsylvania certainly have their share of legends and stories of ghosts and hauntings associated with them. I typically prefer to write about first hand accounts of ghostly happenings in our area. However, as the following tale has been authenticated by many people that have experienced the following phenomenon, I couldn't resist telling the tale of the "woman in white" that purportedly haunts Wopsononick mountain near the city of Altoona, Pennsylvania.

Many years ago, tragedy struck a young couple on their wedding day as they were looking forward to their life together in happiness and bliss. After their wedding ceremony, the happy couple boarded a buggy and, amidst much jubilation from all that attended the holy ceremony, proceeded to travel up Wopsononick Mountain to a motel that was situated on top of the picturesque hillside.

However, as the couple joyfully took in the carriage ride to their honeymoon location, tragedy struck the couple without warning. In an area of the road known simply as the "Devil's Elbow," the carriage in which the newly married couple were riding in, exited the road and tumbled down the

103

edge of the mountain. Unfortunately for the newlyweds, they were both tragically killed in the mishap.

Since the day of this tragedy, numerous people claimed to have seen a ghostly woman in white frantically searching for her long, lost love in various areas of the mountain. Others claim to not only have viewed the ghostly being but, thinking that she might be a person in distress, offer her a ride into the city to obtain help from whatever source that she could find. However, after the young woman enters the vehicle, as they reach the area of the Devil's Elbow, she disappears without any warning to the now bewildered motorist!

Others claim to she the ghostly woman in white carrying a lit candle, apparently searching for something along various areas of road that lead to the top of Wopsononick mountain. Is this poor soul relegated to this earth forever to search for a long, lost love that she will never see again?

It is often said that in an area where a person quickly and tragically loses his or her life, oftentimes the soul or souls that are left behind do not realize that their life has now ended. Could this be the reason that the ghostly woman still haunts the area in and around the Devil's Elbow? And, strangely enough, if this is indeed the soul of the new bride that so tragically lost her life so many years in the past, what of her husband? He also met with death in the carriage crash many years in the past. Where is he? Has he accepted his death and moved on to God while his beloved wife lingers on this earth to search forever for her husband and/ or reasons for their sudden death? Questions such as these enter a person's mind when one looks for answers that would attempt to explain the world of the paranormal. However, until we too become one of the many souls that have left this existence, we are simply left to only wonder.

Strange Happenings At The Cashtown Inn

(Cashtown, Pennsylvania)

The Cashtown Inn, formerly known in Civil War days as the Cashtown Hotel, was established long before the Civil War entered the area around Gettysburg. In 1797, the Cashtown Hotel came into existence and served as a stagecoach inn as well as a tollhouse along what was then known as the Chambersburg Pike.

The Cashtown Inn's original owner, Peter Mark, refused all payment at his establishment with the exception of cash; thus the name of the Inn, and the town, was born.

During Civil War days, Henry Heth's division of A.P. Hill's first corp. arrived at Cashtown on June 29. Brigadier General James Pettigrew and his forces marched the short distance to the town of Gettysburg for reinforcements and supplies but encountered Federal forces moving into the area and thus returned to Cashtown to report his findings to General Heth. On July 1, 1863, Heth's entire division entered the outskirts of Gettysburg from the west to confront Union cavalry. The famous battle of Gettysburg had begun.

The Cashtown Hotel became a Confederate Army command center for A.P. Hill and other Southern leaders as the battle for this northern territory took shape.

Also, this now famous inn was pressed into service as a Civil War hospital during and after the famous battle.

One final note concerning this building that has seen so much history unfold right before its very doors, the Confederate Army, after it was defeated at Gettysburg, retreated through Cashtown on their way over South Mountain and eventually back into Rebel territory.

Today, the Cashtown Inn is a quiet, out of the way must see establishment that many visit for the wonderful food or a quiet night's stay  before they venture onto the Gettysburg Battlefield to immerse themselves in the history of the battlefield and surrounding town of Gettysburg.

However, on occasion, the quiet, peaceful Inn with so many years of history behind it seems to come alive with not only memories of the past but also the restless spirits of the Civil War that seem to demand the attention of selected guests. Many of the reported hauntings that play out at the inn take place during the summer. However, occasional sightings of the paranormal are also reported during the winter months.

Krissy and Valerie Newcomb can certainly attest to the fact that the spirits of the Civil War dead occasionally make their presence known in the off-season for tourism also. As they booked a room in the month of November, they assumed that the spirits of the Cashtown would be at rest during this cold month of the year. However, what they experienced in this late fall month certainly chilled them in a most unique way, a way not soon forgotten by either individual.

While Krissy and Valerie were at the inn, they decided to have a look at various unoccupied rooms on the second floor. Valerie decided to step into what is room #1 on the second floor ahead of her sister. Shortly after Krissy entered the room, under one minute after her sister had entered, she noticed a marked change in the mannerisms and facial expressions of her sister. After inquiring why her sister's mood had changed in a matter of mere seconds, Valerie stated that while she was alone in room #1, the door leading to the room had closed...all by itself! Finding this hard to believe and also attempting to use sound reasoning to explain the closing door, Krissy opened the door in question and again, it closed on its own without any prompting from either guest! As Krissy gently laughed at what was happening, two women hurriedly left room #1 and watched behind them as, again, the door to the room slowly closed on its own! Was there some type of draft or poorly hung hinge on the door that caused it to close?

After this series of unexplained happenings, the two visited the other rooms on the second floor before ascending to the third floor of the historic structure. After viewing the third floor, the two sisters again descended to the second floor and specifically to room #1. This time, Valerie dared her sister to open the door to room #1 again to see if the "ghost" was still in the area. Krissy immediately scolded Valerie and stated that she was looking entirely too hard for something out of the ordinary to happen as they had both heard of the haunting activity at the inn. However, not one to back down from her sister's request, Krissy opened the door to room #1 and both women stood back and watched. All of a sudden, as if the Civil War era spirit was finding this game less amusing than the two girls, the door to room #1 shut one last time. However, this was not the gentle closing of the door that the two had experienced only minutes before. This time, the two frightened individuals watched in great fear as the door to room #1 forcefully shut on its own accord with a loud bang!!! Both left the area and immediately realized that no draft or damaged door hinge could slam a door as they had just experienced!

Many other strange tales have been told over the years of ghostly happenings at the inn. However, the cordial innkeepers only ask that when a tourist visits, whether for a meal, an overnight stay or simply to view the building, please do not ask to "see the ghosts." Please come for the food, pleasant surroundings and/ or the immense amount of history of this grand, old building. Then, if you are one of the chosen few, you might just encounter a Civil War era spirit when you least expect it!

The Cashtown Inn, near Gettysburg
Established 1797

Have you ever experienced a haunting within your home or in any other area of Pennsylvania? If you have and would like to share your experience with various readers, please submit your story to the e-mail address, mailing address or phone number below. Please indicate if you would, or would not like your name included within the text of your story. Every story that is used for publication in one of my offerings receives one free copy of the book in which your story appears in!

Please send your true, personal ghost story and all contact information to:

Mr. LJ Gavlak
PO Box 72
Kylertown, PA 16847
e-mail largav@juno.com
(814) 345-6391

Ghosts! of Pennsylvania

*More interesting reading from the desk of
Lawrence J. Gavlak*

Civil War Hauntings and Beyond
*Ghostly Apparitions Of Gettysburg, Central
Pennsylvania And Other Civil War Sites!*
(Isbn-0-9740357-0-x)

Heavenly Visitors
*True Stories Of Angelic Intervention And
Other Heavenly Encounters*
(Isbn-0-9740357-1-8)

Gettysburg Battlefield Hauntings
Ghosts And Hauntings Of Gettysburg
(Isbn-0-9740357-2-6)

To order copies of these books, please send a
check or money order in the amount of $10 per
book ($8.50 plus $1.50 postage) to:

LJ Gavlak Publishing
PO Box 72
Kylertown, Pa 16847
largav@juno.com

(Pennsylvania residents add 6% sales tax to
total order.)